GO EXTREME!

BE A PRO SNOWBOARDER

By Lynda Arnez

Gareth Stevens PUBLISHING

Please visit our website, www.garethstevens.com. For a free color catalog of all our high-quality books, call toll free 1-800-542-2595 or fax 1-877-542-2596.

Library of Congress Cataloging-in-Publication Data

Names: Arnéz, Lynda, author.
Title: Be a pro snowboarder / Lynda Arnez.
Description: Buffalo, New York : Gareth Stevens Publishing, [2024] | Series: Go extreme! | Includes bibliographical references and index.
Identifiers: LCCN 2023007705 (print) | LCCN 2023007706 (ebook) | ISBN 9781538286999 (library binding) | ISBN 9781538286982 (paperback) | ISBN 9781538287002 (ebook)
Subjects: LCSH: Snowboarding–Juvenile literature. | Snowboarders–Juvenile literature. | Extreme sports–Juvenile literature. | Winter Olympics–Juvenile literature.
Classification: LCC GV857.S57 A765 2024 (print) | LCC GV857.S57 (ebook) | DDC 796.939092 [B]–dc23/eng/20230306
LC record available at https://lccn.loc.gov/2023007705
LC ebook record available at https://lccn.loc.gov/2023007706

First Edition

Published in 2024 by
Gareth Stevens Publishing
2544 Clinton St
Buffalo, NY 14224

Designer: Ellen Weber
Editor: Kristen Rajczak Nelson

Photo credits: Cover, p. 1 Ipatov/Shutterstock.com.com; p. 5 Leonard Zhukovsky/Shutterstock.com; p. 7 Sergey Novikov/Shutterstock.com; p. 9 steba/Shutterstock.com; p. 9 wlablack/Shutterstock.com; p. 9 frco/Shutterstock.com; p. 9 Pixel-Shot/Shutterstock.com; p. 11 Ervin Monn/Shutterstock.com; pp. 13, 25 Dmitry Molchanov/Shutterstock.com; p. 15 homydesign/Shutterstock.com; p. 17 Pavel L Photo and Video/Shutterstock.com; p. 19 lzf/Shutterstock.com; p. 21 GROGL/Shutterstock.com; p. 23 The Camp of Champions Snowboard & Ski Summer Camp/Flickr; p. 27 Iurii Stepanov/Shutterstock.com; p. 29 Daniel Avram/Shutterstock.com; Series Art Mind Pixell/Shutterstock.com; Series Art Duda Vasilii/Shutterstock.com; Series Art PegasuStudio/Shutterstock.com; Series Art Scott Webb/Pexels

Printed in the United States of America

Some of the images in this book illustrate individuals who are models. The depictions do not imply actual situations or events.

CPSIA compliance information: Batch #CS24GS: For further information contact Gareth Stevens, New York, New York at 1-800-542-2595.

CONTENTS

GO FOR THE GOLD!

Chloe Kim started snowboarding at age 4. By 14, she was the youngest gold **medal** winner ever at the X Games! Do you dream of success like Chloe's? Get ready to put in the time and hard work on the **slopes**!

PUSHING THE LIMITS

Pro is short for professional, or someone who is paid to do a sport.

Chloe Kim

GETTING STARTED

Young kids start snowboarding by trying out a snowboard in their backyard, if they live in a snowy place. Many take lessons at ski and snowboard **resorts** or parks. Mastering the basics of snowboarding can take a whole winter season or longer.

PUSHING THE LIMITS

It takes years of work to become a pro snowboarder. Those who really want to get to a pro level spend 100 or more days each winter on the slopes.

There are a few different kinds of snowboarding. Once you learn snowboarding basics, it's time to try them out! Most **competitive** snowboarding is freestyle. That includes halfpipe and superpipe, slopestyle, big air, and rail jams.

PUSHING THE LIMITS

Snowboarding gear—from helmets and goggles to boards and boots—is costly. And, different kinds of snowboarding require different gear.

FREESTYLE SNOWBOARDING

Snowboarders ride over one huge jump and do spins and flips in the air before they hit the ground.

A halfpipe looks like a half tube of snow. Snowboarders ride up and down the pipe. They do tricks when they are in the air at the top of the pipe. A superpipe has the tallest pipe sides.

Snowboarders ride downhill on a course with jumps made of snow.

Snowboarders ride on a rail or something similar and do tricks.

In most competitive snowboarding, completing **impressive** tricks gains snowboarders higher scores from judges. To get to the top of snowboarding, you'll need to learn these tricks. You'll need to come up with some of your own too! This takes practice and time.

PUSHING THE LIMITS

Before pro snowboarder Shaun White retired, or stopped competing, in 2022, he was known for hitting big tricks. In the double McTwist 1260, he would flip twice and do three-and-a-half twists!

Shaun White

FOLLOW THE SNOW!

Pro snowboarders train all year. Many snowboarders move to mountain towns to be near great snowboarding resorts or parks. When it's summer in the Northern **Hemisphere**, they train in New Zealand and Australia! These countries are in the Southern Hemisphere where it's winter at that time of the year.

PUSHING THE LIMITS

The best snowboarders got there by always trying to get better. They try bigger tricks, ride in new places, and work on skills that are hard for them.

CONTEST TIME

You can start competing in snowboarding when you feel ready. Your tricks don't have to be perfect yet! The first competitions you do are good for learning. They show you what you need to work on and what you're good at.

PUSHING THE LIMITS

The best snowboarders compete in the Olympics, the Winter X Games, and national and world championships. But they started with small competitions too!

Michael Cruz at the National Snowboarding Championships

PROS GET PAID!

Snowboarders who win competitions can win money. They also get attention from sponsors! Sponsors are **brands** or companies that give someone money and gear. In turn, the snowboarders **promote** them. Sponsors want winning snowboarders to be seen wearing and using their clothes or gear!

PUSHING THE LIMITS

Anyone who gets paid to do a sport can be called a professional. However, in sports like snowboarding, sometimes "pro" also means that a person competes at a high level in certain competitions.

Aaron March

Some snowboarders get sponsored by sending an edit to a company. This is a video of their best runs and tricks. They can also grow a big social media following. Brands know their gear will be seen by many people.

PUSHING THE LIMITS

At first, sponsors may just send "flow," or snowboarding gear and clothes. Sponsors can also pay for snowboarders to travel to and enter big contests.

IS IT ENOUGH?

Getting paid to snowboard seems like a dream! But, for many pro snowboarders, what they make from prize money and sponsorships isn't enough. They have other jobs. They may teach snowboarding lessons or make and sell art, among other jobs.

PUSHING THE LIMITS

Pro snowboarders must train, compete well, and promote their sponsors—as well as themselves! It can be hard to keep all that up and still work another job.

STAY AT THE TOP

The best-paid snowboarders are often the ones winning the biggest contests. It takes a lot of work to continue to do well! They must keep getting better at the sport. This often means coming up with new or harder tricks.

PUSHING THE LIMITS

Canadian pro Mark McMorris has been known as one of the snowboarders showing off new tricks and ideas. In 2022, he earned his 22nd gold medal at the X Games!

Mark McMorris

Pro snowboarders put their bodies through a lot! They must be very fit to compete well and to keep themselves safe from injury, or harm. From mountain biking to weight training, workouts off the slopes are key to snowboarders staying healthy.

PUSHING THE LIMITS

Pro snowboarders learn to push through practicing hard tricks and the stress, or worries, of competing. They can't spend too much time thinking about falls and failures.

Still, pro snowboarders may not compete for long. Injuries, such as broken bones, can be hard to come back from. Accidents while training can even be deadly. It's important to follow all safety rules when out on a snowboarding run.

PUSHING THE LIMITS

Snowboarders should always wear helmets to keep their heads safe. It could save your life if you fall!

SHOW THE LOVE!

It takes so much time and work to become a pro at any sport! The most important thing is to enjoy every step along the way. Pro snowboarders agree: You can tell when someone loves what they do when you watch them!

PUSHING THE LIMITS

You can start snowboarding now! Talk to your family about finding lessons at a nearby mountain or resort—or take a board into your snowy backyard!

LEARN THE LINGO

bail
getting out of a trick that you know you won't be able to land

corkscrew
a spin that is fast and tight often while in the halfpipe or while freeriding

drop in
to enter a snowboarding run or halfpipe

freeride
to ride through country-like areas or going fast on a snowboarding run

grab
a trick in which the rider holds the edge of the snowboard with one or both hands

jib
to ride a snowboard on surfaces other than snow

mogul
a bump or small hill on the slope

pow
short for powder, or snow that hasn't been touched yet

run
a course or slope to ride on

shred
to ride a snowboard in a really cool and fast way

FOR MORE INFORMATION

BOOKS

Abdo, Kenny. *Shaun White*. Minneapolis, MN: Fly!, an imprint of Abdo Zoom, 2023.

Gish, Ashley. *Snowboarding*. Mankato, MN: Creative Education/Creative Paperbacks, 2022.

WEBSITES

Snowboard
usskiandsnowboard.org/teams/snowboard
Find out more about snowboarding at the Olympics here.

Winter Sports: Sledding, Skiing, Snowboarding, Skating
kidshealth.org/en/kids/winter-sports.html?ref=search
Find some safety tips for taking part in winter sports.

GLOSSARY

brand: A group of products made by a company under a certain name.

competitive: To try to win a contest with others.

hemisphere: One half of Earth.

impressive: Having a lasting effect, or something of very high quality.

medal: A prize given to the winner(s) of a competition. It is often made out of metal and worn on a ribbon around the neck.

promote: To make people aware of.

resort: A place people take a trip to that has activities for visitors to do.

slope: An area of land used for snowboarding or skiing.

INDEX